NORMAN THE DOORMAN

Also by Don Freeman

BEADY BEAR

MOP TOP

FLY HIGH, FLY LOW

THE NIGHT THE LIGHTS WENT OUT

By Lydia and Don Freeman

CHUGGY AND THE BLUE CABOOSE

PET OF THE MET

NORMAN THE DOORMAN

BY DON
FREEMAN

THE VIKING PRESS · NEW YORK

LITHOGRAPHED IN THE U.S.A. BY
HERMER LITHOGRAPHY, INC.

To

Doyle and David

Hilary and Tony

Wiggy and Tuni

Stevie and Sarah

Bernard and Curtis, and

with two pieces of cheese

for my nieces, Donna and Patti

U. S. 1076210

NORMAN THE DOORMAN

In front of a small, well-hidden hole around in back of the Majestic Museum of Art there once stood a mouse named Norman.

Norman was a doorman, and he greeted all the art-loving creatures who came to see the treasures which were kept in the basement of the museum.

"Come right in!" Norman would say to his cousins the Petrinis. "We're quite safe. I've sprung all the traps."

Norman would explain every painting in detail and handle each masterpiece with as much care and respect as if he had painted it himself!

He would also take great pride in pointing out the artistic features of certain pieces of Greek sculpture which rested in the dark corners of the storage room.

Norman's only worry was keeping out of sight of the sharp-eyed upstairs guard, who often came to the basement to set traps for mice!

His bright flashlight frightened the visitors, and
they dashed out the secret hole into the night like
streaks of pink and white lightning.

15

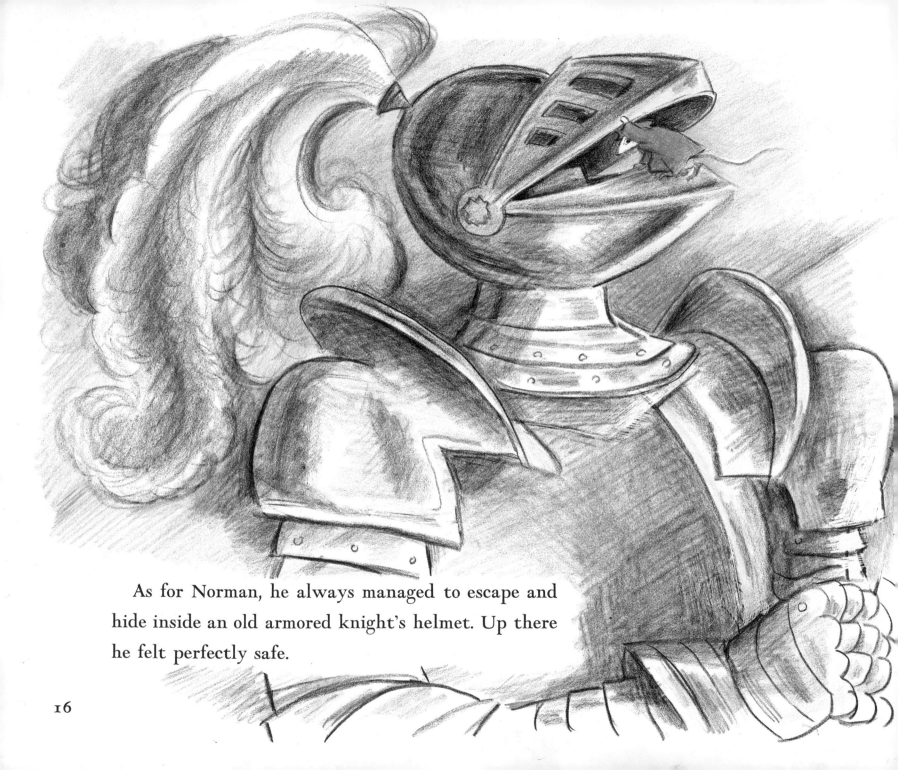

As for Norman, he always managed to escape and
hide inside an old armored knight's helmet. Up there
he felt perfectly safe.

16

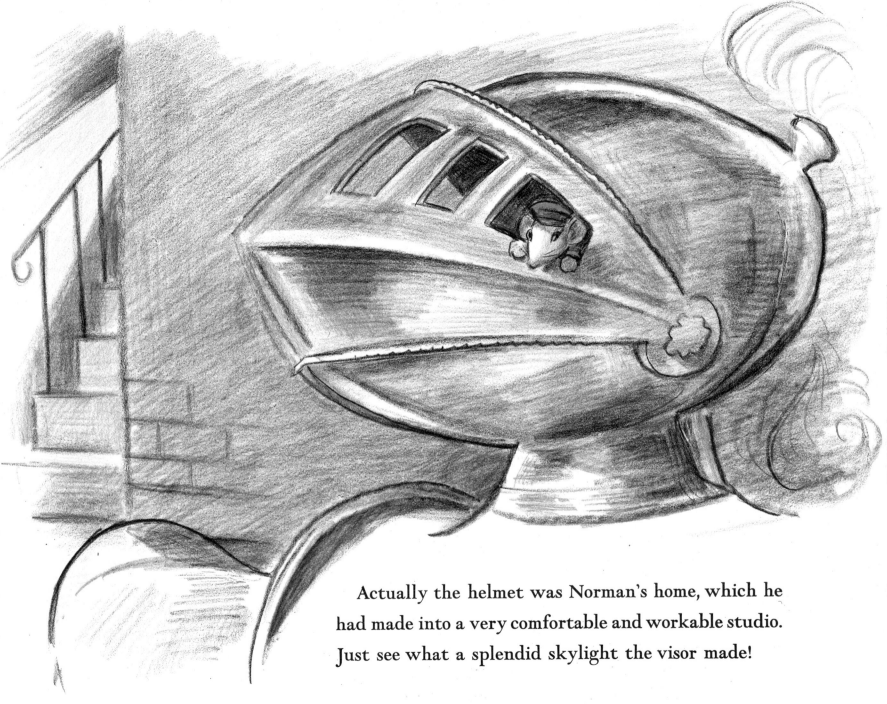

Actually the helmet was Norman's home, which he had made into a very comfortable and workable studio. Just see what a splendid skylight the visor made!

Like most everybody, Norman had a hobby. Each night after work he tried to create something pleasing or beautiful—perhaps a painting of Swiss cheese and crackers, or a statue.

One bitter cold day Norman decided to stay in his studio and make something out of wire. For some time he had been collecting mousetraps and odd scraps of picture-hanging wire, with the intention of putting them to artistic use.

The mousetraps weren't any good any more, since Norman had cleverly taken out the pieces of cheese and then snapped the traps shut without having harmed even so much as a whisker on his nose.

All through the day and far into the night Norman twisted and bent wires into many strange and mysterious shapes—until, at last, he created something

he was really proud of! It looked for all the world
like a mouse on a trapeze.

That night when he finally went to sleep he was
a tired but very happy mouse.

Early next morning when Norman went outside to shovel away the snow in front of his doorway he noticed a man reading a sign nearby.

He too read the sign—

SCULPTURE
CONTEST
OPEN TO ALL ARTISTS,
GREAT AND SMALL!

PRIZES ! PRIZES !

WORKS IN
STONE, IRON, BRONZE, WOOD,
OR WIRE WELCOME

LAST DAY TODAY!

Back he flew!

"Why can't I show my wire statue?" he said as he slid through the visor-lid opening.

But what would he call it? All pieces must have titles, he well knew.

Suddenly he had an inspiration. Stripping off the printed word "TRAP" from the label, and then ripping off the letters "EESE" from the word "cheese," he pasted them together.

Now he had a fitting title for his wire work! Although Norman was a modest mouse, he practically burst a button off his coat.

Then, as this was the last day for the artists to bring their sculpture pieces in, Norman put a cover over his statue, as he had seen the others do, and away he scooted.

Up the front stairway he climbed, one snowy step
at a time.

Once inside the huge museum, he eagerly followed the other sculptors from one room to another. He still had to be extremely careful of the sharp-eyed guard! Contest or not, he didn't want to get caught!

After carefully removing the cover from his wire statue, he left it on the floor with the rest of the contestants' work.

NINA
BY
HIRSCHFELD

Just before leaving, however, he took one last look. Would the judges for the contest notice his "TRAP-EESE"? After all, it wasn't very large.

U.S.1076210

Out he went into the snowy afternoon knowing
he had done his best.

Back once more in his helmet studio, Norman went about sewing new brass buttons on his blue coat. You see, he had not forgotten that he was a doorman who had a job to do.

Meanwhile, upstairs in the Sculpture Gallery of the museum, the judges were busy judging. Quietly and seriously they examined each piece, trying to find which ones deserved prizes.

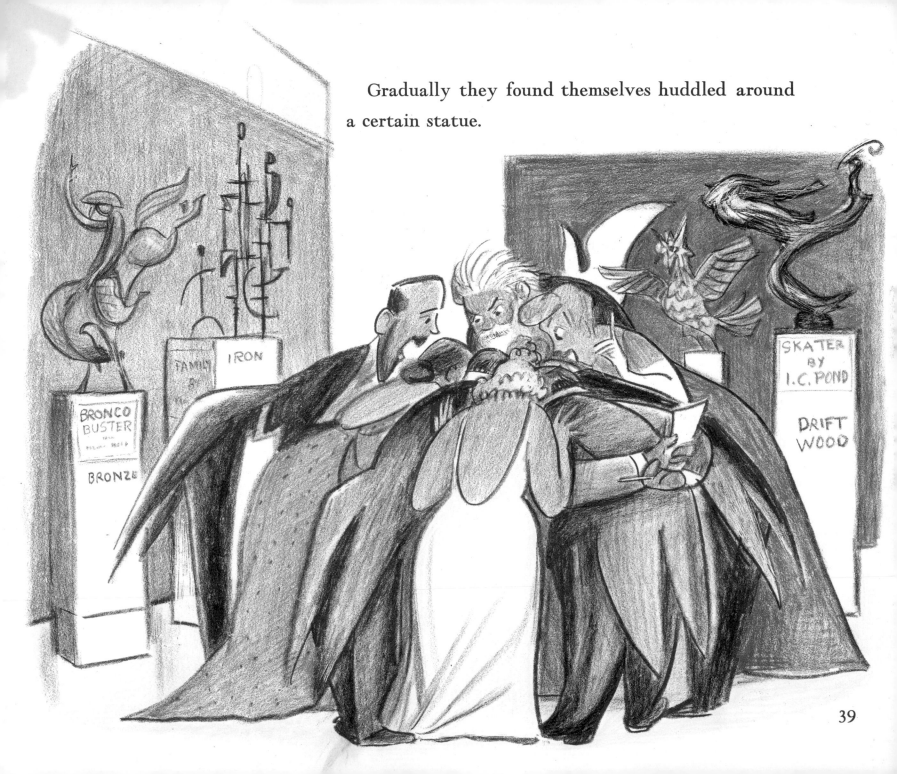

Gradually they found themselves huddled around
a certain statue.

39

"Now *this* is an amazing creation!" exclaimed one of the judges.

"There's no name," said another. "And isn't it a shame it's so tiny!"

"Yes, but remember, the contest is open to great and small," said another judge.

One by one each guard, when asked if he knew who had brought it in, shook his head and said, "No, not I." The Museum director couldn't understand why none of them had caught sight of the artist.

But when the sharp-eyed guard took a closer look he gasped. "Oh, so this is where all my mousetraps have been going! I think I know where to start searching for the tricky trap-snatcher!"

Without waiting another minute, the guard snapped on his flashlight and hurried downstairs to the basement.

"What's this — one of my traps stuck in a knight's helmet?"

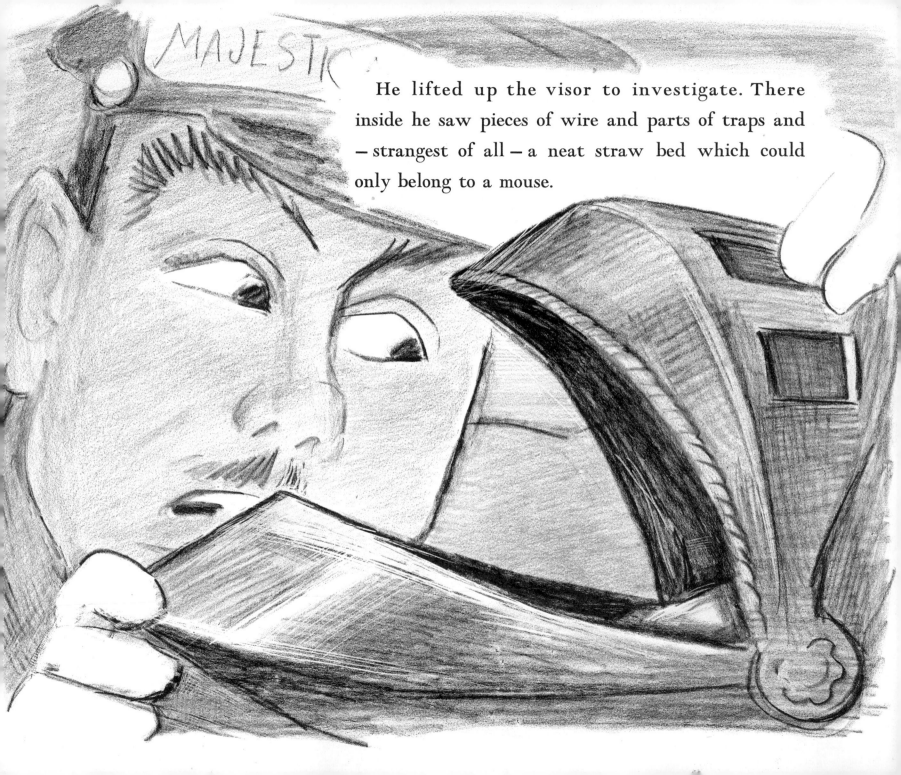

He lifted up the visor to investigate. There inside he saw pieces of wire and parts of traps and — strangest of all — a neat straw bed which could only belong to a mouse.

"Whoever he is, he must be mighty fond of my cheese," said the guard as he knelt down on the floor and pointed the flashlight at some tracks which led out through the hole in the wall.

During all this time Norman had been tending to his duty as doorman. A party of mice from the country, for whom he had been waiting, was long past due, and he was getting mighty cold and hungry.

But, to his suprise, who should be coming around
the corner but the sharp-eyed guard!

"Oho, so there you are!" said the guard as
Norman fled inside.

But when the guard held a piece of cheese just
above the hole and Norman sniffed it, he couldn't
help poking his nose out to get a better whiff.

And just as he was about to reach up and snatch the cheese, a hand came down swiftly and caught Norman by his tail!

"Say, are you the rascal who's been taking my mousetraps every day and using them for artistic purposes?" asked the guard sternly.

"It's just a hobby!" sobbed Norman. "Just my hobby!"

Right then and there the guard tossed Norman up on his shoulders, but he still kept a tight hold on his tail. Norman was sure he was being taken to jail.

You can imagine his surprise when, instead, they entered the museum and heard the artists all clapping and cheering. "Hooray for 'Trapeese'!" they shouted. "Hooray for 'Trapeese'!"

"Well, I'll be bamboozled!" cried the guard. "I do believe you've won a prize! And they're waiting for you to step forward and receive the award!"

The guard rushed up to the judges' platform and said proudly, "Here's the winner! I found him freezing outdoors in the snow!"

"Oh, indeed!" said the head judge, somewhat flustered. "Why, yes—who else could have created the 'daring young mouse on the flying trapeze'? What is your name, my good fellow, and what would you like for your prize?"

"If you please, sir, my name is Norman. I'm the doorman downstairs, and I've always dreamed of seeing the upstairs part of the museum without getting caught. That is what I would like best."

This simple request was granted immediately. Amidst great applause, the guard led Norman out into the Hall, where together they began a grand tour of the entire art museum!

Later that night when Norman returned to his door downstairs he found his mice friends from the country waiting for him there. Of course Norman

invited them into his studio, where he shared with them an enormous slice of Cheddar cheese — a present given him by the kindhearted guard. Oh, what a wonderful way to end the day!

63

Good Knight!

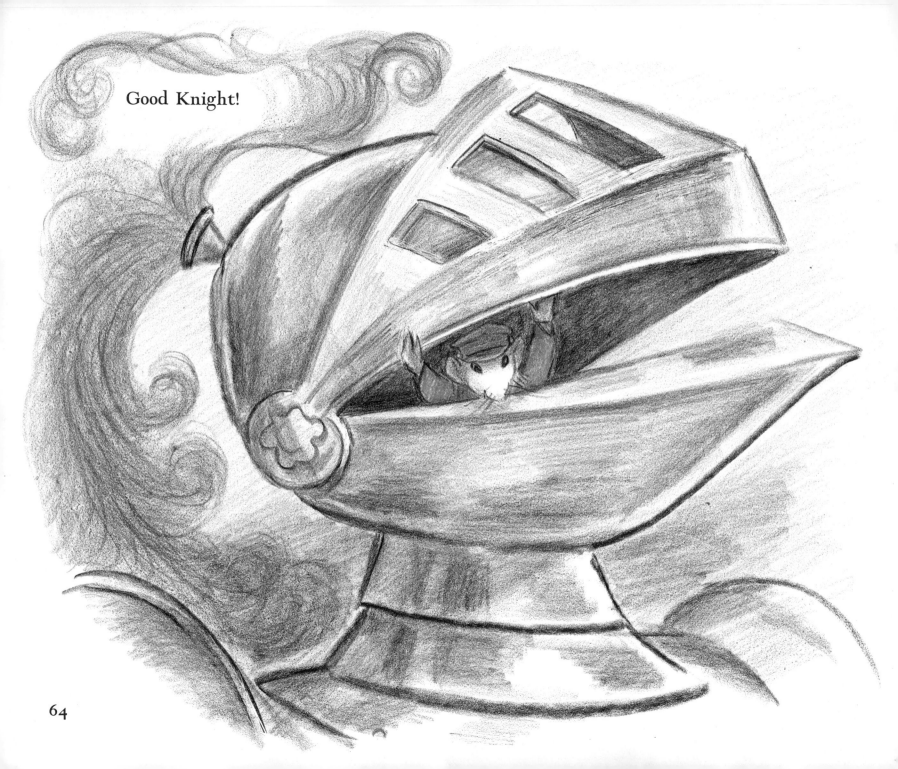

Celebrating the Peoples and Civilizations of Southeast Asia™

THE PEOPLE OF
VIETNAM

Dolly Brittan

The Rosen Publishing Group's
PowerKids Press™
New York

Published in 1997 by The Rosen Publishing Group, Inc.
29 East 21st Street, New York, NY 10010

First Edition

Book Design: Danielle Primiceri

Photo Credits: Cover, pp. 4, 8, 12, 16, 20 © Joe Smolian/International Stock; p. 7 © Archive Photo; pp. 11, 19 © Jeff Greenberg/International Stock; p. 15 © Hollenbeck Photography/International Stock; p. 16 (background) © Joe Smolian/International Stock, (top, middle, bottom) © Cliff Hollenback/International Stock.

Brittan, Dolly.
    The people of Vietnam/ Dolly Brittan.
       p.   cm. (Celebrating the peoples and civilizations of Southeast Asia)
    Summary: Provides a brief introduction to the geography, language, customs, and beliefs of Vietnam.
    ISBN 0-8239-5125-1
    1. Vietnam—Juvenile literature. [1. Vietnam.] I. Title. II. Series.
    DS556.3.B75 1997
    306'.09597—dc21   96-39805
                                                                      CIP
                                                                             AC

Manufactured in the United States of America

Contents

A Land Called Vietnam

Vietnam (vee-et-NAHM) is a country in Southeast Asia. To the north of Vietnam is China. To the west is Laos. And to the east is the South China Sea. In its over 4,000-year history, Vietnam has been known by eleven names. Because of its location and beauty, many countries have fought to rule Vietnam. Each time the country was taken over, it was given a new name. It was first called Vietnam in 1802. *Viet* is Vietnamese for "people," and *nam* means "south."

◀ *The capital of Vietnam is Hanoi.*

The War

In 1954, Vietnam was divided into North Vietnam and South Vietnam. Soon there was another war. Each part of Vietnam looked for help from other countries. The North was helped by the former Soviet Union. The South was helped by the United States. The war lasted for more than twenty years, officially ending in 1975. The North won the war. North Vietnam and South Vietnam became one country again in 1976.

The United States sent soldiers to help South Vietnam fight North Vietnam. ▶

The Language

The people of Vietnam speak Vietnamese. The Chinese ruled Vietnam nearly 2,000 years ago. So the Vietnamese language is in some ways similar to the Chinese language. Like Chinese, Vietnamese is a **tonal** (TOE-nul) language. That means that the same word can mean different things if you change the tone you use to say the word. For example, the word *ma* can mean "mother," "ghost," "horse," or "rice seedling," depending on how you say it.

◀ *Vietnamese children start school at six years old.*
There they learn how to read and write Vietnamese.

9

Religion

Most Vietnamese people follow a religion called **Buddhism** (BOOD-izm). Buddhists are followers of the Buddha, which means "the **enlightened** (en-LY-tend) one." Enlightenment is the complete understanding of life and of your place in life. Many Vietnamese Buddhists also follow two other beliefs: **Confucianism** (kon-FEW-shah-nizm) and **Taoism** (DOW-izm). These are Chinese ways of thinking. They teach that it is important to love others, to respect your parents, and to behave well.

The Vietnamese often light sticks of incense when they offer a prayer to a god. An incense stick is ▶ made of different spices.

3 1833 03600 3942

Homes

Many of the houses in **rural** (RUR-ul) Vietnamese villages are made of bamboo and wood. They have roofs made of tightly woven grass. Around the outside is a bamboo fence for protection. Today, wealthy villagers build brick houses with tiled roofs and glass windows. In **Ho Chi Minh City** (HOH CHEE MIN SIH-tee), most people like to live near their work. Their homes may have two or three rooms, a bathroom, a kitchen, and a small courtyard for drying laundry.

Many houses in rural areas of Vietnam are made of bamboo and wood. The roofs are made of tightly woven grass called thatch.

13

Clothes

Many Vietnamese men wear a **traditional** (tra-DISH-un-ul) suit called an ***ao the*** (ow TUH). Women wear an ***ao dai*** (ow ZY). This is a long white shirt with slits up the sides. It is worn over black or white pants. Many people who live in cities wear high-heeled wooden sandals. Most people who live in villages wear flat sandals or go barefoot. It is important for women to wear hats to protect their heads from the heat of the sun. They are made from palm leaves that are woven into a cone shape.

The cone-shaped hat that many Vietnamese women wear is called a non la. ▶

Getting Around

There are many kinds of **transportation** (TRANZ-per-TAY-shun) in Vietnam. There are large airports, railroads between the main cities and towns, and thousands of miles of roads. Very few people have cars. Some people who live in rural areas ride on water buffaloes. Most people who live in cities travel from place to place on bicycles or motor scooters. Taxis in Vietnam are three-wheeled cycles or three-wheeled motor scooters.

Many people in Vietnam ride bicycles. The three-wheeled cycles that are used as taxis are also called pedicabs or trishaws.

17

The New Year Festival

For the Vietnamese, festivals are more than just having fun. The most important festival is the Vietnamese New Year, called Tet Nguyen Dan. This festival celebrates the start of spring, which is also the Vietnamese New Year. All the members of the family meet for the new year. Houses are decorated with flowers. Colored lights and red and pink banners are hung up in the streets. Children receive gifts or money wrapped in red paper. At midnight, long strings of firecrackers are hung from bamboo poles and set off.

Many Vietnamese people wear traditional clothes during the festivals. ▶

Vietnamese Cooking

White rice is the main part of most Vietnamese meals. It is often eaten with vegetables, meat, or fish, and flavored with spices and sauces. It is said that the Vietnamese have nearly 500 different traditional dishes. Some of these are made with different meats, such as eel, cobra, and bat. Others are made with vegetables. Vietnamese cooking is enjoyed by people all over the world.

This boy is eating his rice with chopsticks and a spoon. Using chopsticks is the traditional Vietnamese way to eat. Chopsticks are often made from bamboo.

Vietnam Today

Vietnam has been ruled by many other countries. The Vietnamese **culture** (KUL-cher) has a little bit of the culture from each of these countries. For example, France ruled Vietnam for about ten years. So many Vietnamese people speak French as well as Vietnamese. But even though there have been so many rulers, the Vietnamese have held onto their own traditions and passed them down to their children. The people of Vietnam are proud of their beautiful country and culture.

Glossary

ao dai (ow ZY) Long shirt with slits up the sides that is worn by
    Vietnamese women over black or white pants.

ao the (ow TUH) Traditional suit worn by men.

Buddhism (BOOD-izm) An Indian religion based on the teachings of
    the Buddha.

Confucianism (kon-FEW-shah-nizm) A Chinese way of thinking based
    on the teachings of Confucius.

culture (KUL-cher) The customs, art, and beliefs of a people.

enlightened (en-LY-tend) Having spiritual understanding.

Ho Chi Minh City (HOH CHEE MIN SIH-tee) Largest city in Vietnam.

rural (RUR-ul) In the country.

Taoism (DOW-izm) A Chinese way of thinking based on the beliefs of
    a man named Lao-tze.

tonal (TOE-nul) Having to do with the tone or sound of something.

traditional (tra-DISH-un-ul) A way of doing something that is passed
    down from parent to child.

transportation (TRANZ-per-TAY-shun) A way of getting from one place
    to another.

Vietnam (vee-et-NAHM) The name of a country in Southeast Asia. It
    means "People of the South."

Index